LAWS OR PLANS

Isaiah of Syria

Translated by: D.P. Curtin

Dalcassian Publishing Company

LAWS OR PLANS

Copyright @ 2009 Dalcassian Publishing Company

All rights reserved. No part of this publication may be reproduced, distributed, or transmitted in any form or by any means, including photocopying, recording, or other electronic or mechanical methods, without the prior written permission of the publisher, except in the case of brief quotations embodied in critical reviews and certain other non-commercial uses permitted by copyright law. For permission request, write to Dalcassian Publishing Company at dalcassianpublishing at gmail.com

ISBN: 979-8-8690-9249-6 (Paperback)

Library of Congress Control Number:
Author: Curtin, D.P. (1985-)

Printed by Ingram Content Group, 1 Ingram Blvd, La Vergne, Tennessee

First printing edition 2009.

LAWS OR PLANS

LAWS OR PLANS

My dearest brother, if you have already left this vain world and given yourself to God, repent of your sins and keep the purpose which you have embraced; and do not listen to your thoughts, when they afflict your mind and say: By no means are your former sins forgiven you; and keep these precepts.

I. Be careful not to eat with a woman, or to enter into fraternity with a boy, or to sleep with a youth on the same floor. When you take off your clothes, don't look at your body.

II. If you are forced to drink wine, do not drink more than three medium glasses: be careful not to break the commandment for the sake of friendship.

III. Do not pay the hourly prayers carelessly, lest you fall into the hands of your enemies. Give as much attention as you can to the meditation of the psalms, because this will save you from an impure life.

IV. Love labor and affliction, so that your passions may be relieved.

V. Guard yourself from lying because it drives away the fear of the Lord. Do not reveal your good deeds to everyone, lest your enemy snatch them away.

VI. Open your sicknesses to your fathers, that you may experience help through their advice.

VII. Compel yourself to the work of your hands, and the fear of the Lord will dwell in you.

VIII. Do not judge your brother when he sins, and do not despise him; for you will fall into the hands of your enemies.

IX. Do not be contentious to establish your word, lest evil dwell in you.

X. Love humility, and do not rest in your own counsel. Let your tongue be accustomed to say: Forgive me, and humility will come upon you.

XI. When you sit in your cell, be anxious about three things: namely, about constant prayer, meditating on psalms, and the work of your hands.

XII. Think to yourself: Of course, I am not alive in this world, except for this day; and you will be delivered from sin.

XIII Don't be hellish, don't let your previous sins be renewed in you. Don't be lazy with your work; and give attention to the meditation of the psalms, and rest will come to you from God.

LAWS OR PLANS

XIV. Force yourself to weep in your prayers, and God will have mercy on you and strip you of the old man.

XV. Know that toil, and poverty, and travel, and affliction, and silence bring humility; but humility forgives all sins. Humility is, that a man should consider himself a sinner and unjust, and not establish his word, and cut off his concupiscence, and fix his eyes on the ground, and bear injury, and labor, and hate, and have honor and rest, and say in all things: Pardon me; but by the grace of humility the enemies are put to flight.

XVI. Be perpetually sad; But if your brothers come to you, you will rejoice with them, so that the fear of God may dwell in you.

XVII. If you travel with your brothers, withdraw from them, that you may be silent; do not turn here and there, but meditate on your psalms and pray to God in your mind. Keep modesty and modesty in all things, and do not extend your hand to those things which are placed before you, except unwillingly.

XVIII. Do not sleep with another person under the same blanket. Pray a lot before going to bed, however tired you are from the journey.

XIX. Do not allow anyone to anoint your body with oil, except for a serious illness.

XX. When you sit down at a table with your brothers, do not eat with pleasure, and stretch out your hand only to what is before you. And let your knees be bent, and do not raise your gaze to another. Do not drink water greedily, nor with noise.

XXI If the necessity of defecating arises when you are sitting among your brothers, get up and throw yourself away from them. Don't be a prostitute among people, and if you have a prostitute, don't let it come out of your mouth and leave you.

XXII. Do not open your mouth to laugh; for this shows that you lack the fear of God.

XXIII. Thou shalt not covet another's thing. If you make a book, do not tear it out, for this shows your affection.

XXIV. If you have sinned in anything, do not be ashamed to confess it, and do not excuse yourself by lying; but bend your knees, and confess your crime, and ask for forgiveness, and you will be forgiven.

XV. If anyone has lied to you, do not be angry, but say: Forgive me, I will not return.

XXVI. Don't be ashamed to ask your teacher.

XXVII. If any one knocks at the door of your cell, while you are sitting bent over your work, leave your work, and take care of his rest.

XXVIII. Do not talk with anyone, and do not pay attention to anyone's words without benefit.

XXIX. If your master sends you on a journey, ask him how to govern yourself, and do according to his command. Do not translate the words. If you guard your eyes and your ears, you will not sin with your tongue.

XXX. If you live with a brother, be with him as a stranger, and do not command him anything, do not make yourself superior to him, and do not act presumptuously with him; and if he commands you something that you do not want, cut off your will, and do not grieve him, lest peace be cut off from you; and know that obedience is greater.

XXXI. If you live with a brother, and he says to you: Cook; say: What do you want? And if he leaves you a choice, cook, because he has come to your hands with the fear of God.

XXXII. When you have risen from sleep, pray before you do any work, and first meditate on the words of God; then to attack the work vigorously.

XXXIII. Meet the stranger cheerfully, and greet him; lest your departure from each other be with loss; and take care that as soon as he comes to you, you ask him questions that are useless to you, but requests from him to pray, and when he sits down, that day: How are you, my brother? and show him some book to read. But if he is tired from the journey, let him rest, and wash his feet. But if he speaks empty words, say to him with charity: Spare me, my brother, because I am weak and am not able to hear these things. But if his clothes were torn, But if he is sick, and his clothes are dirty, wash them. But if he is a wanderer, and there are saints with you, do not allow him to go in to them, but show him mercy and let him go. But if he is poor, do not let him be sad, but give him what God has granted you.

XXXIV. If any brother has deposited anything with you, do not search the deposit unless he is present.

XXXV. If a man leaves you in his cell, and he has gone out, do not raise your eyes to see what is in it, but say to him as he goes out: Give me some work to attend to until you return; and do diligently whatever he has commanded you.

XXXVI. Do not speak with laziness and carelessness; for by this reason, instead of pleasing God, you will provoke him to anger; but stand with fear and trembling, and do not lean against the wall, and do not put aside your feet, that you may stand on one side and stretch out another. Stop your thoughts, and do not allow them to be anxious about carnal things, so that your prayer may be accepted by God.

XXXVII. But if you are present at the mass, guard your thoughts and your senses, and stand before the most high God with fear; that you may become worthy to receive the body of Christ and his blood, and heal your sufferings.

XXXVIII. While you are young, don't wear good clothes until you reach old age.

XXXIX. If you go on a journey with someone older than you, do not go ahead of him. If the elder rises up to address the others, do not lead him to the younger, and remain seated; but stay with him until he orders you to sit down.

XL. When you have entered a city or a town, let your sight fall to the ground, lest the sight of you should be a cause of conflict in your cell.

XLI. Do not sleep in a place where you fear to sin in your heart. Do not eat with a woman or look at her, or even her clothes, if you can.

XLII. If you travel with an old man, do not allow him to carry anything. But if you are young, each one will bear some part. But if it be a little, let each one carry it for an hour, and let whoever carries it go first, and let the sick man take the lead, so that if he is tired and sits down to take rest, you may sit with him.

XLIII. If you ask any old man about your thoughts, open them freely and use them to him whom you trust to keep your secrets; and do not take account of him who is of an advanced age, but who will be refined by learning, work, and spiritual experience, so that you do not report loss if your passions increase.

LAWS OR PLANS

XLIV. Admit that you have many lips at night, that your understanding may be enlightened. Think of your sins, and pray to God for them, and he will spare you.

XLV. If any one accuses his brother of judging you in his presence, even though he is judged by the number of those who judge you, say to him humbly: Spare me, my brother, for I am a sinner and weak, and more subject to what you say, why I cannot hear them.

XLVI. Prefer your brothers in everything, and if any friend has done you honors, say: He has done these honors to me because of you; nor do you taste anything without companions.

XLVII. Don't refuse to borrow something from your request.

XLVIII. Do not often turn your heart to the memory of those whom you have abandoned for the sake of God's charity; but remember death and damnation, and that none of them will be able to help you at that time.

XLIX. If, while you are sitting in your cell, you remember that someone has done you wrong, get up immediately and pray for him in your heart, that God may spare him; for in this way the passion which you suffer because of it vanishes.

L. If you wish to receive the body of Christ, be careful not to harbor anger or hatred in your heart against anyone.

LI. If you were attacked by lust at night, take care not to repeat those aspects in thought during the day, lest your heart be contaminated with pleasure; but prostrate yourself before God, and he will have mercy on you: for he knows the weakness of men.

LAWS OR PLANS

LII. If you give too much attention to fasting and continuous prayer, do not trust that these things will save you; but trust that God will have mercy on the affliction of your body, and will have mercy on your infirmity.

LIII. If you have been seized with an illness, do not let it tire you and let your spirit fail; but give thanks to God that he is concerned about your profit.

LIV While you dwell in your cell, set a predetermined measure for your food, and a set time, and do not exceed it; and give your body as much as it needs, so that it may be able to pray and worship God. But if you have been offered delicious food outside your cell, do not take it to the point of satiety, so that you may be able to return quickly to your cell.

LV. If the devil sows in you a labor which you are not able to bear, do not accept it from them; because they occupy the heart of a man with certain things which he is not able to overcome, in order to wear him down and deceive him. Of course, all their business is without measure and without order.

LVI. Eat once a day, but not to be satiated. Provide your body with what it needs, according to the demands of nature.

LVII. Appoint the middle of the night for prayer, and the other half for the rest of your body. But before you go to bed, watch for two hours in prayer and praise, then give your body rest. If your body slows down while you have to get up for prayer, say to him: Do you want to take rest at this time, and then go to a long punishment? Is it not proper that you labor here a little, and then rest there with the saints forever? For then laziness immediately departs from you, and divine help will come to you.

LVIII. When you have embraced the institution of monasticism, hand over your servant, who, if he wishes to follow monasticism, do not allow him to live with you.

LIX. If you go to sell the work of your hands, do not argue about the price, like worldly people. You will also guarantee the same if you buy anything. Know that the lack of things makes you close to God.

LX. If your brother has deposited any vessel with you, you must not touch it, except by his own consent.

LXI. If any brother asks you to buy him something while you are traveling, do it; but if there be brethren with thee, let it be in their presence.

LXII. If anything has been given to you in return, return it with what you have used; and do not withhold it until it is repeated by you; and if any of that is broken, make amends. If you have lent something to someone, don't repeat it if you know you can't get it back, especially if you don't need it.

LXIII. If he has already left your cell, and you return to him later, and find that some brother is already living there, look for another one; and beware that you do not expel him from there, lest God be angry with you. But if he voluntarily chooses to leave her, you are already justified; But if he has taken anything from his belongings, do not demand it from him.

LXIV. If you wish to leave a room, be careful not to take away any of its furniture, but leave it to some poor brother, and God will provide for you wherever you go.

LXV. The devils rejoice over nothing so much as they rejoice over him who conceals his thoughts from his spiritual master. Do not think that you will become like the Fathers unless you imitate their labors.

LXVI. Keep yourself from riches and from the love of them, because they spoil the fruit of the monk.

LXVII. If you fight against some temptation that has oppressed you, do not give up, but prostrate yourself before God and say: Help me, Lord, because I am weak and am not able to endure this fight; and he will be pleased with you, if your supplication proceeds from an honest heart. If you fight and win, don't boast or trust; but take heed to yourself, since the enemy will devise a more difficult battle against you than before.

LXVIII. If you pray to God, do not say: Lord, remove this from me and grant me this; but say: Lord my God, you know what is more profitable for me, therefore help me and do not allow me to sin against you and perish in my sins, because I am a weak sinner; do not deliver me to my enemies, for I have taken refuge in you; deliver me, Lord, for you are my strength and my hope; and unto thee is power, and glory, and beneficence, and thanksgiving forever. Amen.

The Abbot's Rule of Isaiah is explicit.

LATIN TEXT

Praecepta seu consilia

Frater dilectissime, si jam reliquisti mundum hunc vanum, et Deo teipsum dedisti, poenitentiamage de peccatis tuis, et serva propositum quod amplexus es; et ne auscultes cogitationibus tuis, cum animum tuum affligent et dicent: Nequaquam peccata tua priora tibi condonata sunt; et serva haec praecepta.

I. Cave ne comedas cum muliere, aut fraternitatem ineas cum puero, aut dormias cum adolescente super eadem storea. Cum exuis vestem tuam, ne aspicias corpus tuum.

II. Si ad potum vini coactus fueris, ne bibas plus quam tres scyphos mediocres: cave ne solvas praeceptum propter amicitiam.

III. Ne persolvas horarias preces negligenter, ne incidas in manus inimicorum tuorum. Da operam quantum potes meditationi psalmorum, quia hoc servabit te ab immunda vita.

IV. Dilige laborem et afflictionem, ut leventur passiones tuae. Ne reputes teipsum quidquam in ulla re, et vacabis gemitibus pro peccatis tuis.

V. Custodi teipsum a mendacio quia expellit a te timorem Domini. Ne aperias omnibus tua benefacta, ne rapiat illa inimicus tuus.

VI. Aperi morbos tuos patribus tuis, ut experiaris opem per ipsorum consilium.

VII. Coge teipsum ad opus manuum tuarum, et habitabit in te timor Domini.

VIII. Ne judices fratrem tuum cum peccat, nec despicias illum; incides enim in manus inimicorum tuorum.

IX. Ne sis contentiosus ad statuendum verbum tuum, ne inhabitent in te mala.

X. Dilige humilitatem, et non acquiescas tuo consilio. Assuescat lingua tua dicere: Ignosce mihi et superveniet tibi humilitas.

XI. Cum sederis in cella tua, de tribus sollicitus esto: nempe de assiduitate in oratione, meditatione psalmorum, et opere manuum tuarum.

XII. Cogita apud te: Utique non sum superstes in hoc mundo, nisi hac die; et eripieris a peccato.

XIII. Ne sis helluo, ne renoventur in te priora peccata tua. Ne pigeat te laboris; et da operam meditationi psalmorum, et adveniet tibi requies a Deo.

XIV. Coge teipsum ad fletum in orationibus, et Deus miserebitur tui, et exuet te homine vetere.

XV. Scito, quod labor, et paupertas, et peregrinatio, et afflictio, et silentium afferunt humilitatem; humilitas autem peccata omnia condonat. Humilitas autem est, ut homo reputet seipsum peccatorem, et injustum, et ne statuat verbum suum, et abscindat suam concupiscentiam, et defigat oculos ad terram, et sustineat injuriam, et laborem, et odio habeat honorem, et requiem, et dicat in omnibus: Ignosce mihi; beneficio autem humilitatis fugantur hostes.

XVI. Perpetuo tristis esto; si vero venerint ad te fratres, exhilareris cum illis, ut inhabitet in te timor Dei.

XVII. Si iter feceris cum fratribus, secede ab illis, ut silere possis; nec te convertas huc et illuc, sed meditare psalmos tuos, et ora ad Deum in mente tua Et quemcunque locum ingressus fueris, ne praefidenter agas cum habitatoribus ejus. Serva modestiam, et verecundiam in omnibus, et ad ea quae apponuntur coram te, manum non nisi invitus extendas.

XVIII. Ne cubes cum alio sub eodem stragulo. Ora multum ante cubitum, quamvis defatigatus sis ab itinere.

XIX. Ne permittas ut quisquam ungat oleo corpus tuum, nisi propter gravem morbum.

XX. Cum sederis ad mensam cum fratribus, ne comedas cum delectatione, et extende manum tuam tantum ad ea quae sunt ante te. Et complicata sint genua tua, nec eleves visum tuum ad alium. Nec bibas aquam avide, nec cum sonitu.

XXI. Si excreandi te urserit necessitas, cum sederis inter fratres, surge, et longius projice ab illis. Ne pandiculeris inter homines, et si acciderit tibi pandiculatio, ne hies ore tuo, et deseret te.

XXII. Ne aperias os tuum ad risum; hoc enim indicat tibi deesse timorem Dei.

XXIII. Ne concupiscas rem alienam. Si feceris librum, ne exornes illum, hoc quippe affectum tuum ostendit.

XXIV. Si peccaveris in aliquo, non pudeat te confiteri illud, neque excuses te mendacio; sed genua flecte, et confitere delictum tuum, et pete veniam, et condonabitur tibi.

XXV. Si quis mentitus fuerit apud te, ne irascaris, sed dicito: Ignosce mihi, non revertar.

XXVI. Non pudeat te quaerere a tuo magistro.

XXVII. Si quis pulsaverit januam cellae tuae, dum sedens incumbis operi tuo, desere opus tuum, et cura ejus requiem.

XXVIII. Ne loquaris cum quoquam, nec attendas verbis cujusquam sine utilitate.

XXIX. Si miserit te magister tuus ad iter faciendum, postula ab illo quomodo te regas, et fac juxta mandatum ejus. Ne transferas verba. Si custodieris oculos tuos et aures tuas, minime peccabis lingua tua.

XXX. Si habitaveris cum aliquo fratre, esto cum illo ut peregrinus, nec praecipias illi quidquam, nec te superiorem illi facias, nec praefidenter agas cum illo; et si praeceperit tibi aliquid quod nolles, abscinde voluntatem tuam, et ne contristes illum, ne abscindatur pax a vobis; et scias quod obediens est major.

XXXI. Si habitaveris cum fratre aliquo, et dicet tibi: Coquito; dic: Quid vis? et si electionem tibi reliquerit, coquito, quod tibi venerit ad manus cum timore Dei.

XXXII. Cum e somno surrexeris, ora antequam ullum opus attingas, et meditare prius verba Dei; tunc aggredere impigre opus.

XXXIII. Hilariter occurre extero, et saluta illum; ne discessus vester ab invicem sit cum detrimento; et cave ne statim atque advenerit ad te, interroges illum inutilia tibi, sed postula ab illo ut oret, et cum sederit, die illi: Quomodo vales, frater mi? et exhibe illi librum aliquem legendum. Si vero est defatigatus ab itinere, permitte illi quiescere, et lava pedes ejus. Si autem loquetur verba inania, dic ei cum charitate: Parce mihi, frater mi, quia infirmus sum, et non valeo audire haec. Si autem dissuta fuerint ejus vestimenta, consue illa. Si vero infirmus est, et ejus vestimenta sunt sordida, lava illa. At si vagus est, et fuerint apud te sancti, ne permittas ingredi ad illos, sed fac ei misericordiam, et dimitte illum. Si est autem pauper, ne tristem illum dimittas, sed da ei quod concesserit tibi Deus.

XXXIV. Si quis frater deposuerit apud te aliquid, ne perscruteris depositum, nisi ipso praesente.

XXXV. Si quis reliquerit te in cella sua, et egressus fuerit, ne eleves visum ad perspiciendum quid in ea sit, sed dic ei dum egreditur: Da mihi opus aliquod, cui operam navem, donec revertaris; et quidquid tibi praeceperit diligenter perfice.

XXXVI. Ne ores cum pigritia et indiligenter; hac enim ratione pro eo quod Deo placeas, ad iracundiam eum provocabis; sed sta cum timore et tremore, et ne innitaris muro, nec remittas pedes tuos, ut uno stes, et alium extendas. Obsiste cogitationibus tuis, nec permittas, ut sollicitae sint de rebus carnalibus, ut sit accepta Deo oratio tua.

XXXVII. Si autem adfueris missae, custodi cogitationes tuas, et sensus tuos, et stes coram Deo altissimo cum timore; ut dignus fias, qui sumas corpus Christi et sanguinem ejus, et sanes passiones tuas.

XXXVIII. Dum juvenis es, ne induas vestem bonam, donec pervenias ad senectutem.

XXXIX. Si iter feceris cum majore te, ne praecedas illum. Si assurrexerit major te ad alloquendum alios, ne parvi ducas illum, et maneas sedens; sed sta cum illo, donec tibi ut resideas praecipiat.

XL. Cum urbem aut oppidum ingressus fueris, ad terram dimitte visum tuum, ne visa abs te sint tibi certaminis causa in cella tua.

XLI. Ne dormias in loco, in quo corde peccare times. Ne comedas cum muliere nec aspicias illam, neque etiam vestimenta ejus, si potes.

XLII. Si iter feceris cum sene, ne permittas ut ille portet quidquam. Si autem fueritis juvenes, unusquisque portet partem aliquam. Si vero fuerit modicum, portet illud unusquisque per horam, et praecedat, qui portat, et praeeat infirmus, ut si lassus sederit ad capiendam requiem, sedeatis cum illo.

XLIII. Si quem senem interrogaveris de cogitationibus tuis, aperi illas libere uti se habent ei quem tua arcana servaturum confidis; nec rationem habeas illius qui provectae aetatis est, sed qui doctrina, opere, et spirituali experimento pollet, ne referas damnum, si augeantur passiones tuae.

XLIV. Adnitere ut multum ores noctu, ut illuminetur intellectus tuus. Pensita peccata tua, et deprecare Deum pro illis, et ipse parcet tibi.

XLV. Si quis fratrem suum te praesente judicare apponat, quamvis judicatus ex eorum sit numero, qui te judicant, dicito illi cum humilitate: Parce mihi, frater mi, quia peccator et infirmus sum, et obnoxius illis quae dicis, quare illa audire non possum.

XLVI. Praefer fratres tuos in omnibus, et si quis amicus praestiterit tibi honores, dicito: Propter vos hos mihi praestitit honores; neque gustes quidquam absque sociis.

XLVII. Mutuo aliquid a te postulanti ne deneges.

XLVIII. Ne frequentius corde verses memoriam eorum, quos propter Dei charitatem deseruisti; sed mortis et damnationis memento, et quod nullus illorum eo tempore tibi opem ferre poterit.

XLIX. Si dum sederis in cella tua, memineris quod aliquis tibi male fecerit, surge statim, et ora pro illo in corde tuo, ut parcat illi Deus; ita enim passio quam ejus causa patieris, evanescit.

L. Si corpus Christi sumere velis, cave ne cordi tuo ira aut odium insit contra quempiam: et si quem adversus te iratum noveris, pete ab illo prius veniam, quemadmodum praecepit Dominus noster (Matt. V).

LI. Si oppugnatus fueris noctu a libidine, cave ne cogitatione repetas species illas interdiu, ne delectatione coinquinetur cor tuum; sed prosterne te coram Deo, et ipse miserebitur tui: novit quippe infirmitatem hominum.

LII. Si operam dederis nimio jejunio et continuae orationi, ne fidas quod haec te salvabunt; sed confide quod Deus miserebitur afflictioni corporis tui, et infirmitati tuae opitulabitur.

LIII. Si morbo correptus fueris, ne taedeat te et deficiat spiritus tuus; sed gratias age Deo, quod de tuo emolumento sit sollicitus.

LIV. Dum habitas in cella tua, constitue cibo tuo praefinitam mensuram, et statutum tempus, et ne praetereas illud; et da corpori tuo quantum indiget, ut valeat orare et colere Deum. Si vero oblatus tibi fuerit extra cellam tuam delicatus cibus, ne ad satietatem ex illo sumas, ut cito reverti valeas ad cellam tuam.

LV. Si severint in te diaboli laborem quem ferre non valeas, ne acceptes ab eis; quoniam occupant cor hominis quibusdam rebus quas superare non valet, ut taedio illum afficiant et deludant. Omnia sane eorum negotia sunt sine mensura ac sine ordine.

LVI. Comede semel in die, sed non ad satietatem. Praebe corpori tuo quantum indiget, juxta exigentiam naturae.

LVII. Mediam noctem ad invigilandum orationi decerne, alteram vero medietatem requiei corporis tui. Antequam autem cubitum eas, vigila per duas horas in oratione et laudibus, tum corpori tuo da requiem. Si pigretur corpus tuum, dum ad orationem surgendum est, dicito illi: Visne requiem capere hoc tempore, deinde abire ad longum supplicium? Nonne praestat ut parum hic labores, tum requiescas illic cum sanctis in aeternum? Tunc enim statim recedit a te pigritia, et adveniet tibi divinum auxilium.

LVIII. Cum monachatus institutum amplexus fueris, manumitte servum tuum; qui, si monachatum sequi velit, ne permittas ut habitet tecum.

LIX. Si abieris ad vendendum opus manuum tuarum, ne disceptes de pretio, ut saeculares. Idem quoque praestabis, si quid emas. Inopiam rerum Deo te propinquum facere scias.

LX. Si deposuerit apud te frater quispiam vas, illoque indigueris, ne tangas illud, nisi ipso consulto.

LXI. Si quis frater rogaverit ut illi aliquid emas dum peregrinaris, facito; si autem fratres fuerint tecum, sit in praesentia eorum.

LXII. Si quid tibi mutuo datum fuerit, restitue illud cum eo fueris usus; nec detineas illud, donec abs te repetatur; et si quid illius fractum, resarcito. Si quid mutuo alicui dedisti, ne repetas illud, si noveris illum non posse restituere, praesertim si illo tibi opus non fuerit.

LXIII. Si egressus jam a cella tua, postea repetis illum, et invenies aliquem fratrem jam ibi habitare, quaere tibi aliam; et cave ne illum inde expellas, ne contra te irascatur Deus. At si ipse sponte illam relinquere voluerit, jam justificatus es; si autem acceperit aliquid ex ejus supellectile, ne requiras id ab illo.

LXIV. Si volueris egredi ab aliqua cella, cave ne asportes aliquid ex ejus supellectile, sed relinque illam alicui fratri pauperi, et Deus largietur tibi quocunque abieris.

LXV. De nulla re ita laetantur diaboli, sicuti laetantur de eo qui cogitationes suas spiritualem suum magistrum celat. Ne putes te Patribus similem evasurum, nisi imitatus fueris eorum labores.

LXVI. Serva teipsum a divitiis, earumque amore, quoniam corrumpunt fructum monachi.

LXVII. Si pugnas adversus tentationem aliquam quae te oppressit, ne desistas, sed prosterne te coram Deo, et dic: Adjuva me, Domine, quoniam ego infirmus non valeo sustinere hanc pugnam; et ille opitulabitur tibi, si ex recto corde processerit deprecatio tua. Si certaveris, et viceris, ne glorieris, neque confidas; sed tibi cave, quoniam hostis difficiliorem priore pugnam in te machinabitur.

LXVIII. Si deprecaris Deum, ne dicas: Domine, remove hoc a me, et concede mihi hoc; sed dicito: Domine Deus meus, tu scis quid mihi magis conducat, quocirca adjuva me, et ne permittas ut peccem tibi, et peream in peccatis meis, quia sum peccator infirmus; nec tradas me inimicis meis, quoniam confugi ad te; libera me, Domine, quia tu es fortitudo mea et spes mea; et tibi est potentia, et gloria, et beneficentia, et gratiarum actio in aeternum. Amen.

Explicit Regula Isaiae abbatis.

The Scriptorium Project is the work of a small group of lay people of various apostolic churches who are interested in the preservation, transmission, and translation of the works of the early and medieval church. Our efforts are to make the works of the church fathers accessible to anyone who might have an interest in Christian antiquities and the theological, philosophical, and moral writings that have become the bedrock of Western Civilization.

To-date, our releases have pulled from the Greek, Syriac, Georgian, Latin, Celtic, Ethiopian, and Coptic traditions of Christianity, and have been pulled from sundry local traditions and languages.

Other Selections from the Ancient and Medieval Syriac Church Series:

Writings *by St. Cyprian of Antioch* (Jan. 2009)

Laws or Plans by Isaiah of Syria (Dec. 2009)

The Virtuous Life by St. Isaac of Nineveh (July 2010)

History of the Conversion of the Georgian to Christianity by Marcarius III of Antioch (Aug. 2010)

Four Works by St. Isaac of Nineveh (Oct. 2012)

Life of St. Mary the Harlot by St. Ephrem the Syrian (May 2014)

Fragments by St. Ephraim of Antioch (Mar. 2018)

The Syriac Menologium and Martyrology (Nov 2022)

The Syriac Life of John the Baptist by Serapion the Presbyter (June 2023)

www.ingramcontent.com/pod-product-compliance
Lightning Source LLC
LaVergne TN
LVHW051923060526
838201LV00060B/4156